# THE BOOK OF PRIDDY

## A PHOTOGRAPHIC PORTRAIT OF MENDIP'S HIGHEST VILLAGE

*Albert Thompson*

HALSGROVE
in association with
HTV WEST

First published in 2000 by Halsgrove
Copyright © 2000 Albert Thompson

ISBN 1 84114 086 4


**British Library Cataloguing-in-Publication-Data**
A CIP data for this book is available from the British Library




**HALSGROVE**
Halsgrove House
Lower Moor Way
Tiverton  EX16 6SS
T: 01884 243242
F: 01884 243325
www.halsgrove.com




Printed and bound in Great Britain
by MPG Books Ltd, Bodmin

# Contents

# Acknowledgements

## A COMMUNITY PROJECT

This book contains no original archaeological, geological, historical, or economic thought about Priddy. It is a unique photographic record that is simply the Priddy Family photo album and it is a tribute to the villagers, past and present.

I am grateful to Mid Somerset Newspapers and The Editor of the *Wells Journal*, Estelle Jakeman of the Somerset County Museum Services and the Wells City Museum, Eric Purchase L.B.I.P.P. and Max Jones for permitting the use of Priddy images in their possession.

My particular thanks go to David Irwin, Hilary and Peter Robarts Arnold, and Susie Walker for their valuable assistance and support with sorting and digitising the photos and checking the captions.

Those of us who have compiled this book sincerely acknowledge our debt to the many Priddy folk who have rummaged through attics, old shoe boxes, drawers, photograph albums and digital files and who have so kindly let us browse the contents. This book would not have been possible without their generous and patient help and support. It is the villagers who make the community that is Priddy. This book is dedicated to them; it is part of the continuing story of their village and the people who live and work in it.

*Albert Thompson*

*The List of the Villagers who so kindly loaned the images in their possession:*

| | |
|---|---|
| Geoff Baynes | GB |
| Arthur Blaymires | AB |
| Ms Claire Blaymires | CB |
| Mrs Jenny Davis | JD |
| Roger Dors | RD |
| Ms Chris Dyke | CD |
| Mrs Brenda Finlayson | BF |
| Mrs A Firbank (Mendip Hunt) | AF |
| Nick Furze | NF |
| Mrs Dorothy Gibbons | DG |
| Dave Irwin | DI |
| Mrs Elaine Jenkins | EJ |
| Ian Jennings | IJ |
| Nick Leyton | NL |
| Mrs Clarice Main | CM |
| Mrs Hilda Main | HM |
| Mrs Pam Maine | PM |
| Bevis Miller | BM |
| Dennis Payne | DP |
| Fred Payne | FP |
| Miss Tracey Payne | TP |
| Mrs Betty Payton | BP |
| John Rackstraw | JR |
| Mrs Hilary Robarts-Arnold | HRA |
| Miss Lena Simmons | LS |
| Bob Sparkes | BS |
| Mrs Lesley Sparkes | LS |
| Ashton Sparkes | AS |
| Steve Sparkes | SS |
| Albert Thompson | AAT |
| Mrs Ann Thompson | AT |
| The Wells Museum | WM |
| Mrs Iris Winter | IW |

# Introduction

## PRIDDY

Priddy sits on top The Mendip sheltering in a valley, often shallow and wide as valleys go, that is a major feature of the Mendip landscape. An Area of Outstanding Natural Beauty, the Mendip plateau is haunting and demanding. At 1000 ft, the plateau withstands the weather that sweeps up the Bristol Channel from the Atlantic. Often capped with cloud and shrouded in mist, it faces ancient Avalon and has its own share of myths and legends. Is Priddy the oldest village in Britain, did Christ walk here as a boy? The history of Priddy is almost tangible, with its Circles, Nine Barrows, Ashen Hill Barrows, limestone quarries, gravel pits, lead works and, of course, the Hurdles and ancient Sheep Fair.

The late eighteenth and the nineteenth century saw the blossoming of the Industrial Revolution. The Enclosures Act and the drive for profitable commercial lead mining impacted Priddy's country existence, regulated as it was by the seasons and weather. The early twentieth century saw the price of lead plummet and farming and forestry predominated. In the years after the Second World War's austerities a new affluence germinated and with it new utilities alien to Priddy, electricity from the National Grid and piped water. With this affluence there came a growth in private car ownership and commercial road haulage. The impact of this led to a cut back in Public Transport in the 1960s. No longer did the bus from Priddy Green connect with trains in Wells. By the 1970s the twice weekly bus service had disappeared and at the turn of the millennium the weekly bus hardly provided a meaningful connection with the surviving railheads at Weston-super-Mare, Bath or Bristol. But road traffic within the village had grown, most noticeably at weekends and holiday periods during the summer time. Access to the Mendip landscape, above and below ground as well as from the air above it, became easier and more people enjoyed the leisure activities available or possible in Priddy. By the end of the twentieth century the surviving rural mixed farming on Mendip faced severe economic challenges and the countryside way of life, and its traditions, was under scrutiny. Once remote, the cities and towns surrounding Priddy now press in on all sides and the village forms a rural oasis. But how long before this oasis evaporates?

And so the pattern of life has changed over the last 100 years. Priddy is a village that starts a new chapter of its history and endurance in the twenty-first century. When the Village Hall became a reality through villagers' efforts in October 1949 the village was proud that it could say of itself 'Something Attempted, Something Achieved'. It is this persevering community, with its traditions, self-reliance, and energy, that is Priddy's true beauty. As its uniqueness and setting are challenged from within, as well as from without, it is the community itself that will be tested most. May it have the inner fortitude to continue to 'attempt' and 'achieve' to keep its identity, to cherish its inheritance and be Priddy.

With this in mind what follows is a collection of images ranging over a period from the late 1800s to the year 2000. This collection is not a sentimental expression of an English village; it is an historical record of the resilient community that is Priddy.

The Priddy Friendly Society gathering of the village inhabitants to mark the Club Day in 1901.

# CHAPTER 1

# Priddy Landscape

Priddy is set in an ancient landscape. Clear evidence of continuing habitation exists from Neolithic times. Robin Bush, who was Deputy Somerset County Archivist in the early 1990s, provides a potted history of Priddy in his book *Somerset – The Complete Guide* (published in 1994). A more detailed account of Priddy's historical foundations can be found in Alan Thomas's *The Story of Priddy* (published in 1989 by Ina Books).

A peep into the annals of Priddy is afforded by the following extract kindly supplied by Ted King. It is from 'Historical Notes on Priddy and its Lead Mines' by the Rev. Prebendary J. Coleman taken from a set of *Somerset Archaeological and Natural History Society Proceedings*:

'It may seem strange to read that Priddy was in any way connected with the Abbey or Abbot of Bruere… But among the endowments of this Abbey founded in 1147, by one Nicholas Basset, were lands and pastures at Harptre and Priddy given to it {viz the Abbey} by William, the son of William, and grandson of John, in all probability, a man of Harptre.'

It continues:

'Tradition has it that there formerly stood in the "Priory Field" south of the church at Priddy, a building which belonged to the Abbot, a tradition which is supported by the fact that the grounds, No. 84 and No. 85 on the Tithe Apportionment are named "Prior's Hay" and "Brewers Hill".'

Ted King advises that the parcel of land No. 84 includes much of the present School site. No. 85 is the field entered when climbing over the stone stile in the corner between the School's grass play area, by the Infant classroom, and the Village Hall store. This, Brewer's Hill, is now known by some of the villagers as 'Bruce's Hill'.

Waldegrave Pool in the late 1890s, early 1900s looking through the Scots Pine from the road to the chimneys in the middle background of the Chewton Lead Mines.                                    WM

Waldegrave Pool looking towards the Scots Pines and the road.                                    WM

The Round House in a state of disrepair. It was situated in a field in the lower part of Wills Farm where it borders Nine Barrows Lane. The purpose of the Round House has been lost with the passage of time. Ashton Sparkes, whose father was born at Wills Farm, has an inkling that it was indeed a house of sorts. CM & LS

The Round House before it fell into disrepair during the early 1900s. DI

Rock Cottage at the time that Mr and Mrs Payne lived there. It was this Mrs Payne who gardened Grannies Garden at the top of Nine Barrows Lane with her children and grandchildren.                                    BP

Outside the old Forge, entered from the forecourt of the Queen Victoria Inn, early in the twentieth century with a Mr Payne and a Mr Main. In later years Mr Gilbert Lane lived in the Forge and continued to provide a blacksmith's service alongside his full-time employment. Working horses were his main custom. Hunt horses and riding horse owners used their own blacksmith or a farrier based at Nedge.            CM&LS

Baytree Cottage opposite the fountain in the 1920s before restoration.          DI

A pre-First World War view from behind the houses on Pelting Drove looking across the Village Green.          BS

View of the Vicarage, Church Farm and the Church taken from Coxton End Lane in 1910. Ted King recalls Bertie Weeks calling the lane 'Cock's & Hen's Lane'!          DI

A view looking up the Batch taken in the 1920s. 'Batches' appear in the old
North Somerset coalfield in the Radstock area. Outsiders might call them
coal tips. So 'Batch' appears to be a local name for any short, sharp hill.
There is a field, which is a steep bank, in East Harptree that is called
'Batchey'. DI

A close up of the Vicarage.
DI

Priddy Church of St Laurence and the School in 1950 showing the entrance
before the Village Hall car-park was donated by Albert Main. DI & BS

This postcard is one of a set featuring Priddy in the late 1950s. It purports to show Priddy Pool whereas it is in fact the Mineries Pool which is behind the site of St Cuthbert's Lead Works. Another pool that gets confused with Priddy Pool is Waldegrave Pool on the roadside by Stock Hill and it is alongside the site of Chewton Lead Mines.                    DI

A view looking down past Lower Pitts Farm to Ousel Lodge and Eastwater Cottages in the 1960s.              DI

A view from the field adjacent to the Top Green by the School looking towards Nine Barrows Lane in the 1960s.          DI

Hokerstone Farm, which is by the side of the road leading out of the village
to Townsend, in the 1960s.                                                    DI

Ebborways Farm which was built in 1946, at the
Ebbor Gorge end of the village in Pelting Drove.
                                              CD

Solomon Coombe which was built in 1951, at the
mouth of Solomon Coomb, the combe leading to
Swildon's Hole.                               CD

Priddy Green viewed from above Church Farm.

Three aerial views of Priddy taken by Lt Cdr Albert Thompson R.N. when he was serving on the Naval Air Command Staff at R.N.A.S. Yeovilton. The year is 1982.                    AAT

Looking down on Pelting Drove.

Looking towards Stockhill & Hunter's Lodge.

Warren Farm at Charterhouse, belonging to the Small family, photographed from a
microlight during the 1980s.                                                    GB

A spring morning with the mist rising above the Levels, looking from Deer Leap
across to Wedmore and Sedgemoor in 1988.                                        AB

The Beech Ride, Stockhill, in the late 1980s. Stockhill is the site of the Forestry Commission's Stockhill plantation of fir trees.

CB

An adder in Stockhill woods – one of Priddys oldest inhabitants!

CB

# CHAPTER 2

# Priddy Green

Priddy Green lies at the heart of the village and reflects the passing years. It is not only seen to be the physical centre of the village, with the hurdles on the Lower Green and the Church and School alongside the Top Green, but it is also the location of so much that happens in Priddy throughout the year.

Manor Farm on the Green with Albert Main and members of his family including two sisters taken late nineteenth century or very early twentieth century. Note the flagpole.    HM & JD

Priddy Green as seen from the top of Solomon Coomb in the early 1900s. A road workers' wagon can be seen on the corner of the Green.    PM

Priddy Green again with a road workers' wagon in the background and note the tall hurdle stack. The house below Greenhill Cottage, centre right in the middle distance, was subsequently demolished and the present house, St John's Cottage, built facing the road. Greenhill Cottage was the headteacher's house for the school after the living quarters at the School itself were removed.    DI

THE BOOK OF PRIDDY

Oliver Speed herding his sheep on the Green c.1915/25. He was farming Sugar Loaf Farm on the Batch whilst also having family connections with the New Inn. In early days it is thought that houses could be opened to sell alcohol willy-nilly by hanging a bush outside the front door. The geese on the Green shows that it was used for grazing and animals could roam freely.

GB

Yew Tree Cottage on the Little Batch photographed around 1920 showing Mrs Tom Weeks and some of her children.

WM

Prior to the 1950s the only supply of running water was from the Fountain on the corner of Priddy Green; this view shows the queue for water collection in front of Fountain Cottage.

DI

This is a trip to collect water from the Fountain. Again it shows Baytree Cottage before it was rebuilt.

BS

A postcard of Priddy Green in 1924. LS

Priddy Green in the 1940s taken from St Cuthbert's Farm showing the hurdles with cattle and horses grazing on the common land. HM & JD

Fountain Cottage in the late 1940s with the Church and School on the skyline, and no Village Hall as yet. A railway-style water column has been introduced to ease the collection of water by the villagers – water was not piped in the village until the 1950s. HM & JD

Priddy Green preparing for the Sheep Fair in the late 1950s – note the dilapidated state of the hurdles. The use of the wooden hurdles had been discontinued in favour of hurdles delivered to accommodate the sheep.      DI

No. 2 Pincross. You can just see the outline of a larger opening shown in the stonework around the ground floor window on the left of the front door as you look at it.   In the 1930s No. 2 Pincross was a General Stores and Post Office and this was the shop window. This maybe explains the reason for the post box sited in the side wall of No.1 Pincross.      AT

No. 1 Pincross which the 1885 Ordnance Survey notes as 'Pin Cross'. The derivation of this name is obscure.  But it is known that the sheep wash, a depression on the Green in front of St Cuthbert's Farm, was fed by a watercourse that led from the field opposite what is now Laurel Farm (at the beginning of Pelting Drove).  This may account for the 'cross' – the crossing point over that watercourse.      AT

A view across Priddy Green with Manor Farm in the background in November 1995.     PM

Manor Farm showing the stump of the old flag pole.     PM

The notice board beside the hurdles on the Green explaining: 'These hurdles are a symbolic reconstruction of the original collection which were stored here to form the pens for the Sheep Fair which moved from Wells to Priddy in 1348 at the outbreak of the Black Death. The Fair is now held annually on the nearest Wednesday to the original date of the 21 August.'

SS & AS

Re-thatching the old hurdles one August – the Sheep Fair hurdles are being put up in the background. PM

The hurdles on the Green prior to full restoration in 1997. SS&AS

Restoration of the hurdles in 1997, pushing over the old stack. PM

Restoration of the hurdles in 1997, forming the new base. A time capsule, actually a bottle, was buried under this base. It contains a list of those who took part in the restoration.
*Left to right:* John Davis, Robin Maine, Toby Main and Bill Small.

PM

Restoration of the hurdles in 1997, laying the new hurdles.
*Left to right:* Bill Small, Robin Maine, Toby Main and Pat Small.

PM

The morning after the new stack was built, awaiting the thatcher. SS & AS

The new stack with Manor Farm in the background and showing the debris. The old hurdles were auctioned at a Friendly Society event in August 1997.

SS & AS

The new stack of hurdles looking towards Manor Farm and the Batch.

SS & AS

The new stack with St Cuthbert's Farm, Pincross and the village telephone box in the background.

SS & AS

Since the 1980s the Friendly Society has been providing a Christmas tree on the Green which always looks most cheerful, especially when it is enhanced with the appropriate weather. Carols are sung by village people around the tree on Christmas Eve.

AT

Another seasonal view of the Christmas tree on the Green. GB

# CHAPTER 3

# The Church

The Church is a continuum that stretches across the centuries, reflecting birth, life and death and the rotating seasons. Refurbished in the late 1800s, it has been cherished throughout the twentieth century, with the refurbishment of its lead roof and its bells recommissioned for the new millennium with the addition of two new bells.

The Church is presently referred to as St Laurence within the joint parishes of Westbury-sub-Mendip, Easton and Priddy. However, it is listed as St Lawrence in the Diocesan Register of churches. Robin Bush, in *Somerset – The Complete Guide*, and Alan Thomas, in *The Story of Priddy*, both provide historical evidence for this latter name.

Four photographs of St Laurence Church, Priddy (two of which are on the following page). The reverse of these cardboard originals have an inscription stating 'as before restoration 1880'. It is not clear if this is the date when the photographs were taken, or the date when restoration took place.

*Above and right:* Views from the south-east and north-west sides of the Church showing the state of neglect and disrepair. Note the missing pinnacles on the front of the tower.

HM & JD

*Above and left:* Views inside the Church showing the east and west ends of the nave. In the view to the altar note the Jacobean rood screen and the central lectern. These survive. A casualty in the restoration of the Church was the use of the stone pulpit, here shown as still in use and which was originally the entrance to a long-removed rood loft. A wooden pulpit on the north side is now used. Also the south transept shows the Church before the organ was built. The view to the tower shows the water damage in the north-west corner. It was not until the lead roof was renewed in the 1970s that this dampness was finally conquered. HM & JD

The War Memorial in Priddy Church as it was erected after the First World War. After the Second World War the name of Emrys Russell, Sgt Air Gunner, was added.                    BP

Priddy Church c.1910, much improved as a result of its restoration.          DI

Priddy Church c.1920.                                                   DI

## Church of St. Lawrence, Priddy

### PARISH MAGAZINE

#### OCTOBER, 1956.

PRIEST-IN-CHARGE : REV. J. T. GEORGE, M.A.

DIOCESAN LAY-READER : MR. ROBERT HILL.

CHURCHWARDENS : MR. A. MAIN, MANOR FARM, PRIDDY.
MR. B. WEEKS, "EASTVILLE," PELTING ROAD, PRIDDY.

SIDESMEN. MR. J. MAIN, SOLOMON COMBE, PRIDDY.
MR. R. DYKE, LOWER PITTS FARM BUNGALOW.

PAROCHIAL CHURCH COUNCIL.
TREASURER : MR. C. LINHAM, 3, TUCKER STREET, WELLS.
SECRETARY. MRS. B. GROVES, WELLINGTON FARM, PRIDDY.
EX-OFFICIO. MR. A. MAIN, MANOR FARM, PRIDDY.
MR. B. WEEKS, "EASTVILLE," PELTING ROAD, PRIDDY.
ELECTED. MR. A. WEEKS, MR. J. MAIN, MR. R. DYKE, MRS. K.
DYKE, MRS. H. MAIN, MRS. E. RENDALL, MRS. M.
SPARKES. MR. R. DYKE. (MRS. D. B. FIELD CO-OPTED)

MOTHERS' UNION. ENROLLING MEMBER : MRS. GEORGE, THE VICARAGE, CHEDDAR.
SECRETARY AND TREASURER : MRS. E. RENDALL, PELTING ROAD, PRIDDY.

ORGANIST : MR. C. LINHAM, 3 TUCKER STREET, WELLS.

SACRISTAN : MRS. J. MAIN, SOLOMON COMBE, PRIDDY.

SUNDAY SCHOOL : MISS K. RIGGS, LOWER PITTS FARM BUNGALOW, PRIDDY.

CHURCH CARETAKER : MRS. G. WEEKS, "CREPON," PRIDDY.

SCOUT MASTER : MR. R. DYKE, LOWER PITTS FARM BUNGALOW, PRIDDY.

MAGAZINE SECRETARY : MRS. D. B. FIELD, ROCK COTTAGE, PRIDDY. TEL. 311

The cover of the Parish Magazine for the Church of St Lawrence for October 1965. At that time Priddy was under the Parish of Cheddar. The magazine showed the receipts for the Priddy Parish Church Fête held on the 28 July 1956. A total of £114 15s 3d was taken and after an expenditure of £38 1s 8d a sum of £76 13s 7d was available for Church funds. The expenditure included a sum of £5 0s 0d for a pig, being the prize for the highest score in the week-long skittle competition.                LS

Mrs George, the Vicar's wife, opening the Church Fête in 1959. The two lads to the left of Mrs George are Raymond Price and Douglas Groves. Also in the picture are Evelyn Randell, Pat Groves (now Pat Small the wife of Bill Small), Mrs Mabel Payne, Christine Main, Jenny Gadd, Krista Muench and Chris Dyke.

HM & JD

Priddy Village Fete in 1961 outside the School. Chris Dyke is with her pony, Prince, and Liz Beecham and Gill Lane are on board.

CD

Children in fancy dress at the Church Fête outside theVillage Hall in 1963. Includes Andrew Sherrel, Alma Sparkes (in the back), Chris Dyke, Gill Lane and Linda Payne.  CD

Church Fête fancy dress in 1963.
*Back, left to right:* Linda Payne, Gill Lane, Helen Sherrel.
*Front, left to right:* Penny Sparkes, Carol Body, Wesley Lane.  CD

Church Fête fancy dress in 1963 including Edric Hobbs, Gill Lane, Helen Sherrel, Sally Lane, Penny Sparkes, Carol Body and Wesley Lane.                                                                                                      LS

Vernon Sparkes on the bottle stall at Priddy Church Fête in 1966. With him is his daughter, Penny Sparkes, now Penny Tucker.    LS

Priddy Village Church Fête on the Lower Green in 1972. At that time the local Liberal Party would hire a marquee on the Lower Green and hold a dance on the Friday night. The cost of the marquee would then be shared with the Church who would hold their Summer Fête on Saturday afternoon, going on until the early evening with skittles.    CD

Priddy Village Church Fête in 1972 showing the Friendly Society swing boats which make an appearance in almost all outdoor village events. CD

Michael Main in the stocks at the Church Fête on the Top Green in 1981. PM

Nick Furze in the stocks at the Church Fête, Silver Jubilee year 1977. AT

The Church Walk in 1986 showing Tom Medlicott, Lucy Davis, Rachel Dors and Iain Thompson. It is an event that happens spasmodically over the years and always much enjoyed by those who take part. Ted and Anne King originally mapped the routes. NF

Rev. Michael Wynes in the Village Hall being presented with a stereo radio on his retirement in 1986. With him are Mrs Hilda Main (People's Warden) and Mr Bob Dyke (Vicar's Warden). HM & JD

The St Francis Window in the Children's Corner of St Laurence Church. This was put in by Ivor and Dorothy Gibbons in memory of their daughter, Catherine, who died on 6 October 1988 aged nineteen. It was made by Fran Davies who lives and works in Stoke St Michael. St Francis of Assisi was chosen because of Catherine's love of animals and in particular her pony, Fingle.     DG

Catherine Gibbons with her pony, Fingle, in the garden of Eastwater Farm where she lived.     DG

A view taken from the Church Bell Tower looking over the School and Village Hall roofs to the Green. In the late 1980s the Bell Tower was opened on the day of the Church Fête.　AB

A view taken from the Church Bell Tower looking towards the Nine Barrows.　AB

The Church bells, in the late 1980s, frapped down.　AB

In March 1996 the original three bells in St Laurence Church were joined by a fourth dated 1845, which came from a redundant church at Compton in Surrey in 1995. The bell was collected from Eayre and Smith, Bell-hangers and Engineers at Melbourne in Derbyshire, and taken to Bob Parker, Priddy's bell-hanger, at Taunton. The bell was then sent on to the Whitechapel Bell Foundry in London to be re-tuned to match in with the existing three bells in the Tower. In May 1996 a fifth bell dated 1889 was also fitted. This bell came from a church in Gosport, Hampshire and was also re-tuned by Whitechapel Bell Foundry and fitted by Bob Parker. The original three bells are very old, one dated 1613 and another 1618 and it is believed that these also came to the village second-hand, possibly from Glastonbury. The current project is to replace the old wooded frame with a galvanised steel frame, and re-fit and re-hang the original three bells.

The original three bells. IJ

Nick Furze overseeing Bob Parker and his assistant taking the bell out of the car at the foundry in Taunton in 1995 and in 1996 the bell arriving at the Church. IJ

The bell being hung in 1996.

IJ

The group of Bell Ringers in 1996.

*Left to right:* Nick Furze, Fred Payne, Alison Moody, Tim Large, Ruth Glass, Simon Glass, Ian Jennings, Phil Romford.

IJ

The fifth bell being put into place in 1996.                                IJ

Bob Parker's assistant putting the fifth bell into the new frame.          IJ

Dedication of the new bells in St Laurence Church on 15 September 1996.

*Left to right:* Bob Dyke Church Warden, Rev. Ewan Macpherson Parish Priest, The Venerable Dick ('Dick the Deacon') Acworth Archdeacon, and Robin Maine Church Warden. Robin follows a long tradition of Mains as Church Wardens.          PM

St Laurence Church, Priddy, in 1996 on a perfect winter's day. Compare the Church now with the 1880 pre-restoration photographs.                                                           IJ

The candlelit Nine Lessons and Carols Service in Priddy Church in 1996.                                PM

Robin Maine and Alex Barlow taking the plough into Church for blessing at the Plough Service in 1996.

PM

The Christmas Crib made by Jack Phillips and Michael Main, his grandson, is put in the Children's Corner of Priddy Church every year.     PM

The 1st Priddy Scout Banner laid up in the Church 9 August 1998 having been in the care of Bob Dyke, the last Scout Leader/Scout Master.     CD

Carol singing round the village in 1999 on a trailer pulled by a tractor driven by Robin Maine. This tradition is organised by Pam Maine each year with help from Iris Winter and others.     PM

# CHAPTER 4

# The School

Priddy School began life in 1854 and was run by the National Society for Promoting Regligious Education. Priddy was considered very lucky to have a school prior to the Education Act of 1870, which made education compulsory for children between the age of five and thirteen. Public funding of the School dates back to the founding of the Priddy and St Cuthbert's Out School Board in 1877.

Enid Williams, who took up her first teaching appointment in the 1920s at Priddy School, recalls

'There were three classes, I took the middle one, sharing the main classroom with the Headmistress. A large stove with "Slow But Sure" carved on its stomach heated the room, often festooned with drying garments and heating drinks. There was no school transport or school meals, one little family tramping 5 miles each way over the lonely endless green undulations of the hills. The girls wore pinnies and the boys heavy boots and long corduroy trousers.'

Priddy School in the early twentieth century, showing the toilet block that existed at that time.    DI

Priddy School in 1912. The first girl back left is Elsie King and the last boy front right is Seymour King.    LS

Priddy School during the 1920s.
*Left to right, back row:* R. Payne, Wilf Sparkes, ?, Stan Beecham, Lawrence Dors, Maurice Winter, Frank Sparkes, Les Gadd.
*4th row:* ?, Grace Rodgers, Georgina Lane, May Russell, Wyn Weeks, Hilda Voke, Phyllis Weeks, Ida Weeks, Rene Weeks, Mabel Rodgers, Miss Mullen, Miss Mullett.
*3rd row:* Mary Bishop (with May Russells hands on her shoulders), Eadie Rodgers, Ruby Speed, Elsie Lovell, Phyllis Pyke, ?, ? Rodgers, ? Herridge, Miss Reeves.
*2nd row:* In this row are Arthur Speed, Welwyn Champ (?), Ted Simmons, Ern James, Clifford Lane, Ashton Sparkes, Windsor Champ, Dan Weeks, Albert Hillard, Stan Russell, Cyril Winter, Ern Young.
*Front row sitting:* George Gadd, George Bishop, ?, Betty Hyman, Kathleen Main, Althea Saunders, Ruth Champ, Phoebe Speed, Iris Champ, Gerty Pollard, Emrys Russell, ?, Gilbert Main or is it Ken Payne ?, ?, ?.
The Sparkes are probably the family that Enid Williams referred to, coming into Priddy from Castle Farm each day.                                                                                                           BS

Priddy School in the early 1920s.
*Left to right back:* George Collier, Hilda Voke, ?, Madelaine Weeks, Norah Weeks, Ethel Sparkes, Terry Paxton, Fred Hares.
*Middle:* Miss Reeves, ?, ?, Rene Weeks, Winnie Weeks, Edna Weeks, ?, ?, Eddie Gadd, Jack Main.
*Sitting:* Wilfred Sparkes, Lawrence Dors, ?, ?, Maurice Winter, Wilfred Pitman, Ted Hares.                    HM & JD

Priddy School in about 1927 dressed for a performance.
Miss Mullett, a teacher, is at the back.  She lived in the stores, run by her father and mother, by Eastwater Cottages near the corner by Lower Pitts Farm.  In the picture are Frank Sparkes, Walter Hares, Ruby Speed, Ashton Sparkes, the Spakton girls, Rene Weeks, Leslie Gadd, Arthur Speed, Elsie Speed, Daniel Weeks, Clifford Lane, Dolly Saunders, Cyril Winter, Jim Speed, Bill Rose, Phyllis Pyke, Phyllis Hares, Miriam Bishop.      IW

Priddy School  in about 1929/30 including many familiar names:
Gladys Payne, Gertie Pollard, Cyril Winter, Toby Main, Welwyn Champ, Ruby Gadd, Phyllis Pyke, Ruby Speed, Miriam Bishop, Bill Dallimore, Kathleen Main, Ken Payne.  The little girl marked with an X third from the right in the second row is Lena Simmons.                              CM & LS

Priddy School in about 1970.

IW

Priddy School in 1971 with Headmistress Mrs Finlayson.
*Left to right back row:* Mrs Finlayson, Alun Jenkins, ?, Jeremy Barnes, ?, ?, Stephen Main.
*3rd row:* ?, ?, Stuart Kerton, ? Godfrey, Heather Gibbons, Ginette Pole, Giles Mullis.
*2nd row:* Helen Simmons, ?, Jackie Bown, ? Groves, ?, Gary Pole, Chris Winters.
*Front row sitting on the floor:* ?, ?, ? Groves, ?, Steven Gibbons, Robert Briely.

PM

The village children who participated in the Silver Jubilee celebration party in 1977.          FP & TP

Priddy School Juniors Class in 1982.
*Left to right back row:* Glen Humber, Daniel Groves, Alton Hobbs, Lee Sparkes, Iain Thompson, Thomas Brookes, Richard Leyton, James Furze, Mrs Finlayson, James Vicarage.
*Front row:* Tracey Payne, Lucy Davis, Inga Hobbs, Deborah Squires, ?, Rachel Dors, Imogen Neale.          AT

Priddy School in 1984 with David Gunter, the Headmaster, and Beryl Newberry, the Infant Teacher.

HRA

Beryl Newberry, the Infant Teacher at Priddy School with her class in 1987.

NF

Priddy School c.1988 with Mr David Gunter and Mrs Beryl Newberry.

HRA

Priddy School 1999 with Gina Harris as Headmistress.

EJ

Priddy School on Miss Riggs' retirement day in 1965.                    LS

Miss Riggs was the Infant Teacher at Priddy School from 1946 to 1965 and during all that time she lodged with the Dykes and lived as a member of the family, cycling to the School each day. There is a picture in the Church given in her memory.                    CD

Priddy School Staff in 1975/76.
*Left to right:* Jenny Davis, Sylvia Sparkes, Valerie Barnes, Iris Winter, Brenda Finlayson, Joyce Bird and Wendy Lucas.                    HM & JD

Priddy School Staff in 1982.
*Back left to right:* Sylvia Sparkes, Joyce Bird, Iris Winter, Florence Thorpe.
*Front left to right:* Jenny Davis, Brenda Finlayson, Beryl Newberry.

IW

Brenda Finlayson's retirement day in July 1982. She had been Headmistress at Priddy School since April 1969. Included in the photograph are Debbie McGaw, Iain Thompson, Glen Humber, Lucy Davis, Deborah Squires, Lee Sparkes, Thomas Brookes, Matthew Pearson, James Vicarage, Lawrence Potter, Richard Leyton, Dean Sparks, Tracey Payne, Imogen Neale, Rachel Dors, Inga Hobbs, Zoe Humber, Amanda Chivers, Daniel Groves, Alton Hobbs, James Furze, Joseph Mett, Adam Butterell, ? Medlicott, Katie Potter, Caroline Chivers, Jenny Watson, Gemma Butterell, James Chivers, Thomas Medlicott, Sowena Andrews, Helen Payne, Rachel Nest, Daniel Moysey.                    BF

Priddy School on the evening of Mrs Finlayson's retirement showing Robin Maine presenting her with gifts.　　BF

Mrs Joyce Bird's retirement as Priddy School's Caretaker on 31 August 1986. Iris Winter, David Gunter, Gerald Bird, Joyce Bird, the gentleman who delivered the school meals, Florence Thorpe, Sylvie Sparkes (in background Hilda Main, Mary Davis). *Sitting on the floor:* Jenny Davis, Tilly Joskey, Beryl Newberry.　　IW

Priddy School's young Recorder Ensemble, including Gill Lane, Trudy Payne, Chris Small and Sally Lane on the Chime Bells.

CD

Priddy School Recorder Ensemble.
*Left to right:* Linda Payne, Chris Dyke, Susan Foxwell, Ann Churches, John Smart, Glynn Snelgrove, Richard Weeks, Alan Bird, John Denley.

CD

Priddy School Ensemble.
*Left to right back:* Trudy Payne, Helen Sherrell, Andrew Foxwell.
*Front:* Penny Sparkes, Gill Lane, Sally Lane.

LS

Priddy School Gymnastic Display, between the School and the Village Hall by the gateway to the Church, in 1970 – note no gate or wall around the school field.    PM

The boy is Chris Winter at Priddy School in c.1970.

IW

Stuart Baynes at Priddy School in 1970/72.

GB

Priddy School Sports Day on the Top Green, Mothers' Race in the mid 1970s
*Left to right:* Penny Butterell, Judy Baynes (who always won), ?, Ann Thompson and Pauline Leyton.   NF

Priddy School Sports Day in 1996.
*Left to right:* David Gunter, Quinn Miller, Camilla Hares, Craig Hares, Judy Andrews, Lucy Andrews, Judith Weeks, Shanta Miller.   PM

Maypole dancing in the 1930s with Lena Simmons and Anthea Saunders among others.   CM & LS

A group photograph of the Maypole dancers in c.1971.                                    GB

Maypole dancing at Priddy School with Mrs Finlayson, the Headmistress, in the
background c.1971.                                                                                          GB

Priddy School Camps were begun in 1984 by David Gunter, the Headmaster, when Priddy School swapped with another school in North Devon. They then moved to Freshwater East in Pembrokeshire. David was usually accompanied by Nick Furze, Marion Chivers and Karen Andrews and the week was always enjoyed hugely.

Priddy School Camp 1985. NF

Priddy School Camp party in the mini-bus in 1986. NF

Priddy School Camp in 1986. NF

Priddy School Camp in 1987/88.  NF

Priddy School Camp in 1987/88. NF

Priddy School Juniors Nativity Play in 1976. The picture includes Helen Dors, Alyssa Hobbs, Keith Payne, Christopher Thompson, Barry Payne, Michael Main, Martin Owen.

FP & TP

Priddy School Pantomime, *Cinderella*, including Tracey Payne, Inga Hobbs, Jo Thompson, Jane Murrell, Peter Murrell, Nicola Baynes, Lucy Davis, Lee Sparkes, Iain Thompson, Katherine Furze, Daniel Butterell, Ben Butterell. Wendy Lucas, the Infant Teacher, started pantomimes with younger children in 1976. She also put on Nativity plays.

FP & TP

Priddy School Nativity Play in 1973.                                    PM

Priddy School Show sometime in the late 1950s.
*Left to right:* Krista Muench, Ann Smart, Chris Dyke.

CD

Priddy School Show during the late 1950s
*Left to right, back:* ?, Keith Gadd, Denis Payne, Lyn
Fudge, Susan Main, Evelyn Rendall.
*Front:* ?, Linda Payne, Chris Dyke, ?, Shirley Gadd, ?,
Sarah Organ.                                      CD

Priddy School Show – *A Midsummer Nights Dream* c.1957. The teachers at the time were Mrs Fudge and Miss Riggs. *Left to right:* Sarah Organ (in the tree), Jenny Main, Robert Neale, Jenny Green, Doreen Groves, Krista Muench, Chris Dyke.

CD

Priddy School United Football Team in 1981.
*Left to right back:* Christopher Boddington, Dean Sparkes, David Gunter, Daniel Groves, Richard Leyton.
*Front:* Alton Hobbs, Glen Humber, Lee Sparkes, Iain Thompson, Laurence Potter.

AT

The School group taken during the week of centenary celebrations, for the formation of the Board School. For a whole week in October 1977 staff, children and parents dressed as they would have in 1877. Everyone took part and joined in with the spirit of the time and great fun was had by all. Mrs Finlayson brought out the records book in class and meted out punishments in the appropriate style when occasion deserved. A parade around the village formed part of the week and there was a special service in the Church to which the Vicar, Rev. Michael Wynes, invited the previous incumbent, Rev. Dennis Smith, to speak. The children had a party and a cake with a hundred candles. On the last evening there was a party in the Village Hall just for the adults and Mrs Finlayson was presented with a lovely plant and flowers.

*Left to right back row:* Mrs Tilly Joskey, William Simmons, ?, Mark Kerton, Darren Barnes, Jason ?, Barry Jenkins, Mrs Brenda Finlayson, Mrs Wendy Lucas.
*3rd row:* Kelston Price, ?, Helen Dors, Sarah Edwards, Keith Payne, Tina Pole, ?, Michael Main, Catherine Gibbons, Rosalind Bateman, Richard Leyton, James Chivers ?.
*2nd row:* Michael Owen, Rachel Dors (standing), Kevin Sparkes, Martin Owen, Alyssa Hobbs, Richard Bateman, Andrew Weir, ?, ?.
*Front row:* Alton Hobbs, ?, Inga Hobbs, Elliot Davis, Lee Sparkes, ?, Nicola Baynes, Deborah Squires (behind Nicola), ?, Debbie Lewer, Catherine Furze, Jane Murrell, James Vicarage, Daniel Butterell, Gemma Butterell, Ben Butterell, Lucy Davis, Tracey Payne.

BF

Priddy School Centenary Parade around the village in 1977 led by Brenda Finlayson.                    BF

Priddy School Centenary Party in the Village Hall to finish off the week's celebrations. *Left to right those present include:* Kathleen Dyke, Bob Sparkes, Bob Dyke, Lena Simmons, Alma Sparkes, Vernon Sparkes, Roger Dors, Ashton Sparkes, Penny Sparkes, Jack Main, Mr Smith, Brenda Finlayson, Judy Baynes, Phyllis Sparkes, Mrs Garvin, Nick Leyton, Jenny Davis, Pauline Leyton, John Davis, Robin Maine, Christine Mullis, Pamela Maine, Norman Mullis (?), Veronica Furze, Jim Finlayson. In the front are Mike Bown?, Nick Furze, Alan Thomas, Geoff Baynes.                    BF

These seven children are thought to be Priddy School leavers in 1956 being photographed in Robin Maine's field next to the School. *They include:* Jenny Gadd, Douglas Groves, Pat Fairman and Evelyn Brierley.

CD

# CHAPTER 5

# The Village Hall

The History of the Village Hall goes back to the immediate post Second World War years. Any Priddy gathering requiring a hall, such as a dance or an entertainment, took place in the School. The absence of a village community meeting point was resolved when a suitable prefabricated building was acquired, erected and fitted out as a Village Hall. The Hall was opened on 28 October 1949. Over the subsequent years it has been expanded and its facilities updated on several occasions. Managed by the Priddy Village Hall Committee it really is 'something attempted, something achieved'.

The Priddy Gay Nineties First Birthday party in September 1949. This was held in the School as the Village Hall was not ready. The name Gay Nineties was a universal name for Old Time Dance Clubs. Priddy's Dance Club lasted until the 1970s and was greatly enjoyed. The picture includes, in the front, Dick Muir, Ron Payne, the gentleman from Westbury who supplied the music, and Bob Dyke. In the middle are ? Young, Mrs Lane, ? Young, Kathleen Dyke, the Rev. OHoran (?), Bill Moore. In the background right is possibly May Sparkes (wearing glasses). CD

The opening of the village hall was quite a celebration.

Children's fancy dress.                                          IW

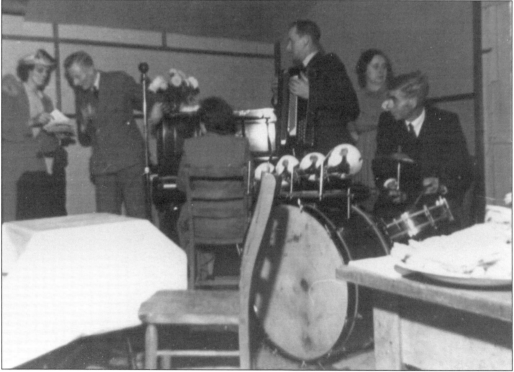

The Dance Band and the indications of a buffet.                 IW

Dressing up as cowboys and cowgirls in 1949 raising funds for the new Village Hall.

Joan Williams.    IW

Reg Payne and Ellen Fowler.    IW

Gilbert Lane.    IW

A very early 1950's event in the new Village Hall. It was certainly spring and cold to judge by the flowers and the top coats. Behind those seated at the table are the Rev. Lord, Mrs Ben Dors, Mrs Lane, Mrs Hewish. *Seated facing:* Walt Weeks (?), Robert Dyke Snr, Mrs Dyke, Mrs Rendall, Mrs Gadd, Tommy Gadd, Cecil Linham, Mrs Bolton, Nellie Weston, Bill King, Mrs Fowler, William Harvey, Viney Main, Bert Russell, Mrs Blodwyn Russell (hidden), ?. *Seated opposite:* Wilf Hewish, Alfie Lovell, Mrs Payne, Henry Payne, ?, Bertie Weeks. *Standing are:* Mrs Lord, May Sparkes.

BS

The same 1950's event viewed from the other end. Seated on the left the additional faces, obscured on the right in the previous photograph include Mrs Lovell, Mrs Julia Dors, Mr Rendall.  BS

Twenty-first anniversary of the Village Hall in 1970  the Beer Quality Tasting Committee
*Left to right:*  Grace Weeks, Mrs Holder, Elsie Speed, Phyllis Holder.        HM & JD

Twenty-first anniversary of the Village Hall in 1970.
*Left to right:* Sylvia Hobbs, Grace Weeks, Jacky Dors, Margaret Lane, Pauline Denley (now Leyton),
Jenny Main (now Davis) cutting the cake, Kathleen Dyke and May Sparkes.        HM & JD

An early event showing the Village Hall in use in the 1950s and among those recognised are Maurice and Iris Winter in front of the door in the background, and Ray Dunford seated on the right with Trevor Dunford on his lap.                                    CM & LS

Harvest Supper late 1970s, early 1980s. Michael Wynes, the Vicar, did a lot to revive the Church during his time at Priddy and Nick Leyton and Nick Furze restored the Harvest Supper (which had been begun by Hilary Thomas) in 1976 to the very popular event it still is each year. Mr and Mrs Williams are seen seated to the right of the table.                 NF

Harvest Supper in the Village Hall.                 NF

Nick Furze leading the community singing at the Harvest Supper during the early 1980s, with David Gunter, the School's Headmaster playing the piano in the background.                                                NF

Nick Furze and Bill Thorpe in full flow with the community singing at the Harvest Supper during the early 1980s.                                                NF

Children holding up their Cycling Proficiency certificates in 1980/81 with their parents and P.C. Jerry Brice in the Village Hall. The Police Inspector came to do the testing and the presentation.
*Left to right back:* Bob Murrell, Fred Payne, Tom Owen, Roger Dors, Jerry Brice, John Rackstraw, Albert Thompson , Arthur Blaymires, Nick Furze.
*Next:* Chris Thompson, Barry Payne, Rachel Dors, Keith Payne.
*Next:* Catherine Gibbons, Jane Murrell, Inspector Dean?, Jo Thompson, Alissa Hobbs.
*Front:* Matthew Person, Antony Rackstraw, Martin Owen, Michael Owen.                                                JR

Priddy Flower Show in the 1990s. This was put on by the Village Hall Committee and organized for them by Phil Grace (centre) and her team of helpers. Bob Sparkes is seen receiving a prize from Robin Maine whilst Anne and Ted King look on in the background.　PM

*Above left:* A village Family Christmas Party in the Village Hall including Catherine Furze, Nicola Baynes, Tracey Payne, Matthew Pearson and Ben Butterell.　NF

*Above right:* A village Family Christmas Party in the Village Hall including Veronica Furze, Jonathan Pearson, Catherine Furze, Bob Dyke and Ashton Sparkes.　NF

*Right:* Bob Faxon dressed as Father Christmas.　NF

Some special events in the Village Hall

Jack and Hilda Main's Ruby Wedding Celebrations in the Village Hall. Left to right: Mr Hildick, Mrs Pam Maine, Mr Jack Duck, Mrs Sylvia Hobbs, Mrs Muriel Duck, Mr Stan Hulin, Mrs & Mrs Jack and Hilda Main, Mr Bob Sparkes, Mr Bob Dyke, Mrs Ivy Hulin, Mrs Kathleen Dyke, Mrs May Sparkes, Mrs Sylvia Sparkes. HM & JD

Priddy Old Time Dance Club's Twenty-first Birthday Party with Iris Winter helping to cut the cake. Dance Clubs were very popular in Priddy and all around the area. Clubs took it in turn to host an evening of 'Open Nights'. Amongst those in the picture are: Mr Walton, Maurice Winter, Mary Davis, May Sparkes, Iris Winter, Janet Payne, Bill Moore, May Birge, and Florence Thorpe. IW

The Village Hall decorations in preparation for the Silver Jubilee Celebrations in 1977.     JR

The Queen's Silver Jubilee Children's Party held in the Village Hall in 1977.  Among the children are Judy Rackstraw, Ben Butterell, Antony Rackstraw, Daniel Butterell, Catherine Furze, James Furze.     NF

Village children at the party to celebrate Prince Charles' and Lady Diana's wedding in 1981. CD

A children's party in the Village Hall to celebrate the wedding of Prince Charles and Lady Diana in 1981. Seated on the left hand side can be seen Peter Leyton, Katie Potter, Paula Dyke-Garfield. CD

# CHAPTER 6

# Priddy's Pubs

The pubs in Priddy reflect the changing local community as well as society. The Hunter's Lodge is a traditional wayside inn that once served those who laboured at St Cuthbert's Lead Works and which now draws the caving community. The Queen Victoria served the village and was the meeting point for the Friendly Society, had a well supported Folk Night in the 1970's and is now a family pub catering for rambler, caver, tourist and villager alike. The New Inn also slaked the thirst of the hard-working villagers and has grown into an inn with bed and breakfast, meals and facilities for special occasions. The Miner's Arms was a Guest House and it grew into a restaurant venue with a world-wide reputation for its Mendip specialities. As 1999 drew to its close, so did the Miner's close.

From wayside hostelry, to a hub of village life, to a place of relaxation, from a haunt of working men, to a place where families can eat out, Priddy's pubs march with the times.

The Hunter's Lodge c.1890 before the thatched roof burnt off in 1900. The proprietor at that time was Samuel Weeks who can be seen in the cart.

RD

A group outside the Hunter's Lodge, probably on the closure of the mine in 1908. Includes Tommy Gadd, Arthur Payne, Rueben Speed and Mark Lovell who was Iris Winter's grandfather and Foreman at St Cuthbert's lead works.                     RD

The Hunter's Lodge c.1914/18 showing the bottom building with the missing roof replaced with one sloping backwards. The present proprietor, Roger Dors, replaced the pitched roof in 1965. Ernest Beacham was the proprietor at this time and he used the bottom building for his business as a wheelwright/cartright and timber dealer.     RD

The Hunter's Lodge c.1920-30 with a new tiled roof replacing the thatch and two charabancs and a delivery lorry parked outside. The proprietor at this time was Joseph Chapman Dors.     RD

The Hunter's Lodge c.1930s.
*Left to right:* Mr Fotterill from the Wells Estate, Mr Hobbs from Penn Hill Farm, Francis Dors (Joseph's son), Julia Dors (Joseph's wife), Joseph Dors (proprietor and Roger's great uncle) and John (Jack) Dors who was Joseph's father and Diana Dors' great grandfather.     RD

The Hunter's Lodge c.1930s with Joseph Chapman Dors, proprietor. P.C. Pring is approaching the group sitting on a bench outside the inn.            RD

A group of people drinking cider outside the Hunter's Lodge with Joseph Chapman Dors on the right who was the proprietor from 1900 until 1946.            RD

The Hunter's Lodge c.1952 when the proprietor was Joseph Benjamin Dors. A Model A Ford YD 9041 is parked outside.
RD

The Hunter's Lodge in the late 1950s/early 1960s before the lavatories had been built and the front porch added. The carts and bicycles of yesteryear have been replaced with cars and motorbikes.

DI

The Hunter's Lodge early to mid 1970s. Proprietor is Roger Dors. Note the addition of the porch and lavatories where the old cart shed used to be.

RD

The Castle of Comfort at the turn of the last century. WM

The back of the Miner's Arms Guest House c.1950. DI

The Miner's Arms' kitchen, lounge and dining room in 1961 when it was bought from Mr and Mrs Murrell by Lt Cdr Leyton and his wife. At the time there were some very interesting paintings on the wall which in the end proved too expensive to insure so they had to be removed. When the Leytons took over the restaurant they made it very famous for their speciality dishes of snails and the Priddy Oggie. They also set up a food mail order business of frozen pre-cooked dishes and tinned foods which were sold all over the country. They also brewed their own ale and were known as the smallest brewery in the country, and, with CAMRA, began the trend for small breweries. They kept the Miner's Arms until 1974.

NL

A copy of the Mendip/Priddy snail recipe, taken from page 68 of *British Cooking*.

NL

A copy of Roy A. Denly's milk invoice from when he and his wife May supplied milk from their farm to Priddy, including the Miner's Arms.

NL

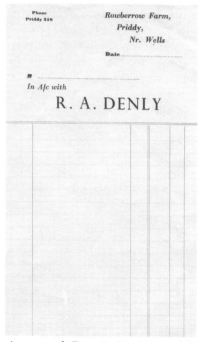

The Miner's Arms in 1968.

NL

The Queen Victoria Inn became an inn in 1851 whilst in the ownership of Elijah Bishop. Prior to that it was two separate buildings, probably a cottage and a barn, or even two cottages and a barn. During this time running an inn was invariably a secondary occupation and land that went with the property would be run as a farm or smallholding. Photographs throughout the period show a variety of boards and it is a belief that the term Queen and a picture of her head was prohibited during her lifetime and for several years after her death – hence Victoria Inn. However, the 1885/86 Ordnance Survey maps show the buildings as Queen Victoria Inn.

Elijah Bishop sold the pub to Berryman Burnell and Co., brewery, and it remained in the hands of the brewery's successors until 1975 when the present owner, Geoff Baynes, bought it. The extension at the end of the main house, to the left, was converted by the brewery just after the War from a barn to lavatories. The short part of the L to the right of the main house, housed the cellar downstairs, while upstairs was used by the Friendly Society as a meeting room. Now downstairs forms part of the bar area and upstairs is part of the domestic accommodation.

A copy of the inventory and valuation of the fixtures, fittings, stock-in-trade, etc., taken over by Mr John Sparkes at the Queen Victoria Inn in 1919.

SS & AS

Kate Winter and family outside the Victoria Inn in 1903. The smaller board below that pronoucing Victoria Inn Charlton Beer Ales & Stout clearly shows Queen Victoria Inn above the name of the licensee.                    IW

An early twentieth century photograph of customers at the Victoria Inn with their mugs of cider – note the two handles – and their clay pipes. The fireplace at that time was built with bricks and in two sections, one being for stacked logs. This fireplace replaced the original and was itself subsequently replaced with a modern one. However the present owner, Geoff Baynes, returned the fireplace to its original glory.    GB

The Victoria Inn sometime between 1915 and 1925 whilst Maurice Voke was landlord.    GB

Hilda Main (née Voke) outside the Victoria Inn during the late 1930s when her mother was landlady.    CD

Outside the Victoria Inn during the 1930s with Bert Russell, Fred Bethel and Jack Saunders.  BS

The Victoria Inn in the 1940/'50s, with a Morris Van parked outside.  GB

A photograph of Bob Sparkes' family taken outside the Queen Victoria Inn during the 1950s.

BS

Outside the Queen Victoria Inn, Bert Russell is on the left.  BS

Geoff Baynes, the Queen Victoria landlord, drawing a pint and showing chicken and baked potato on sale for 5/-. GB

Transformation of the Queen Victoria began in 1982 and was completed in 1983. GB

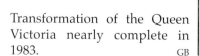

Transformation of the Queen Victoria nearly complete in 1983. GB

The Queen Victoria in 1985.                                    AT

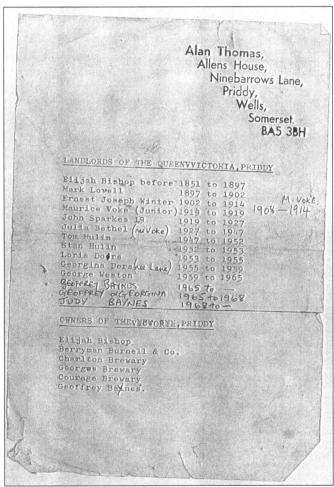

Alan Thomas,
Allens House,
Ninebarrows Lane,
Priddy,
Wells,
Somerset.
BA5 3BH

LANDLORDS OF THE QUEENVVICTORIA, PRIDDY

Elijah Bishop before 1851 to 1897
Mark Lovell                1897 to 1902
Ernest Joseph Winter 1902 to 1914        M.VOKE.
Maurice Voke (Junior)1919 to 1919    1908—1914
John Sparkes 19        1919 to 1927
Julia Bethel (née Voke) 1927 to 1947
Tom Hulin               1947 to 1952
Stan Hulin             1952 to 1953
Loris Do>rs            1953 to 1955
Georgina Dors(née Lane) 1955 to 1959
George Weston          1959 to 1965
GEOFFREY BAYNES        1965 to —
GEOFFREY & GEORGINA    1965 to 1968
JUDY  BAYNES           1968 to —

OWNERS OF THE VICTORIA, PRIDDY

Elijah Bishop
Berryman Burnell & Co.
Charlton Brewary
Georges Brewary
Courage Brewary
Geoffrey Baynes.

A list of the landlords and owners of the Queen Victoria
Inn.                                    GB & Alan Thomas

Leo Garvin, a Danish gentleman who lived with his wife at the Vicarage, in 1957/58 outside the New Inn.

NL

The New Inn sign naming Emily Speed and the late Oliver Speed as licensees.

NL

Phyllis Pyke in the 'cellar' of the New Inn.

NL

Nick and Pauline Leyton being served through the hatch at the New Inn in 1969.                     NL

In front of the fire at the New Inn with a poster in the background advertising the election of the first ever Priddy Parish Council.                     NL

Leo Garvin on the settle which he bought from the New Inn (along with the clock and a picture showing the Boer War) when the inn was taken over by Fred Owen.                     NL

The Priddy Eight skittles team – the League winners in 1991.
*Left to right back:* Mike Bown, Rex Steer, Frank Booth, John Davis, Alan Stott.
*Front:* Mike Malcolm, Roger Cook, John Stott, Tom Owen, Peter Jones.

JD

# CHAPTER 7

# Priddy Weather

'Everywhere on Mendip the air is remarkably pure, but on these heights it is even more invigorating'. *Somerset*, Maxwell Fraser (GWR Publication, 1934).

Basting the Badger. The story behind this is not known but it is known that badger was eaten and the meat is somewhat like pork. Will Jackson who was a Mendip Huntsman used to eat it at an inn in Cornwall. Perhaps it was a seasonal occurrence. LS

The snow in the winter of 1939.
DI

Four postcards of the deep snow in the winter of 1939.

WM

The snow in Priddy in January 1939 looking towards Priddy from Townsend.                    LS

*Above clockwise:* Snow in Priddy during the winter of 1963 in the eastern end of the village. Looking towards Stockhill from the Hunter's Lodge. Breaking through a snowdrift at the bottom of Eastwater Lane near Lower Pitts to allow the sheep to get through to Lower Pitts Farm. The corner of the road to the village viewed from the entrance track to Lower Pitts Farm. The sheep squeeze through.                    CD

Steve and Sharon Sparkes in the winter of 1963 near the Miner's Arms.                                    SS & AS

Liz Blaymires with daughter, Claire, outside their home in Pelting Road viewing a snowdrift in 1978.

AB

Snow fills Pelting Road, which has been variously known as Pilton Drove, Pelting Drove or Pelting Road during the twentieth century.

AB

Snow in Eastwater Lane in the winter of 1980/81, with Judy Baynes travelling by the only sensible means – skis!　　　　　　　　　　　　　　GB

Arthur Blaymires skating on the Chewton Mendip Lead Mine pool, Waldegrave Pool, in 1981. The pools here regularly froze up during the winter but in latter years it is a less common occurrence.　　　　AB

An example of hurricane damage at Stockhill in 1984.　　　　　AB

Christmas Day 1993 snow in Dursdon Drove looking towards Deer Leap.　　AB

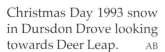

Priddy Green viewed through the trees at Laurel Farm in 1996.                              AT

View towards Rose Farm from the Forge in the New Year of 1996.

AT

Mendip winter wonderland after the ice storm, 19 December 1999.

SS & AS

# CHAPTER 8

# Priddy and War

From pre-First World War and the summer military encampments, to the formation of the Mendip Company of the Home Guard with its Priddy Platoon and the arrival of the Land Army in the Second World War Priddy has had its brush with war throughout the twentieth century. The nearby ranges, that serve the Territorial Army, and the airspace above, designated over The Mendip for military low level flying training, still provide regularly their own peculiar sound bites of gunfire on the night air, the instant roar of a passing fighter, and the whirr and clatter of circling helicopters.

Four postcards depicting the North Somerset Infantry Yeomanry Camp at Priddy in 1907. In the pre-First World War years the camps were, it appears, annual events.          DI

The Scottish Rifles on Priddy Green in 1910. Soldiers would camp regularly in Priddy during the summer on military exercises.

GB

This picture of one of the regular pre-First World War Army Camps is interesting when it comes to determining where the photograph was taken. The 1885/86 Ordnance Survey maps indicate three locations where it would have been possible to get such a view with the Barrows on the horizon and walled fields in the foreground. Do the ruined houses and the continuous wall across the photograph indicate a road? If so the location could have been either towards the top of East Water Lane looking across the lane towards the Barrows (Ashen Hill or Priddy Nine Barrows), or, the rise in the field either side of Lower Pitts Farm Bungalow (now Badgers Wood) looking towards the Barrows, or, the rise in the field opposite Fairladywell looking across and to the left towards the Barrows. To the compilers of this book, the alternative that seems most likely is from one of the fields by Lower Pitts Bungalow. If it were taken from this position either two ruined properties existed on the village side of Cold Comfort, or Cold Comfort was a ruin. If the latter, it was to be rebuilt twice.

DI

A postcard, front and reverse, sent from a soldier who was encamped with his unit in Priddy in August 1910. Wet summers are not something new to Priddy! DI

The Mendip Company Home Guard in 1944.

CD

The Priddy Platoon Mendip Company Home Guard in 1944. This included Henry Dyke, Ashton Sparkes, Arthur Payne, Bob Dyke, Maurice Winter and Charlie Packer who ran the group. Charlie worked for Yeoman Quarries which were started up after the First World War and employed soldiers who left the services. It was his expert knowledge of explosives that was so useful in the Home Guard.

CD

Land Girls' Hostels in St Cuthbert's field facing the Green. They were later turned into housing and then pulled down in about 1965. IW

Rose and Olive who were Land Army girls in the 1940s billeted in the Hostel at Priddy, with Bob Sparkes outside Fairladywell. BS

As a keepsake, in gratitude for friendship shown, Rose sent this picture of herself to May and Bert Sparkes. She is wearing the formal Land Army uniform. BS

Emrys Russell, who joined the R.A.F., and Bob Sparkes outside Fairladywell. Sergent Air Gunner Russell, who flew Lancasters based in Holland, was sadly lost in Service.
BS

In the years when our Country

was in mortal danger

ROBERT DYKE

who served 7 June 1940 - 31 December 1944

gave generously of his time and

powers to make himself ready

for her defence by force of arms

and with his life if need be.

*George R.I.*

# THE HOME GUARD

Bob Dyke's Service Commendation for the Home Guard, signed by George VI.  CD

# CHAPTER 9

# Priddy Industry
## Mining, Farming and Forestry

Newcomers to Priddy often wonder where its heritage lies. Certainly Mining, Farming and more recently to a lesser extent, (in manpower if not in area) Forestry are parts of the answer. The underlying factor was, of course, economic – the ability to generate income. For example, in the sixteenth century the mining area was split into four 'Liberties'. Each of these four Liberties of Mendip had its Lord Royal who appointed agents known as 'Lead Reeves', to whom the miners were required to pay the 'Lead Lot' a tythe of one-tenth of the miners' output. The Lead Lot was collected twice a year on Lady Day and again at Michaelmas.

The Lords Royal and their Liberties were:

Lord Richmont – Smithan Hill
The Waldegrave Family – Chewton Mendip
The Bishop of Bath & Wells – Priddy
The Abbot of Glastonbury – Charterhouse

Priddy Lead Works showing two chimneys, the date unknown.                                        WM

Priddy Lead Works showing Minories House on the left and The Beeches on the right.          WM

Chewton Lead Works beyond the Waldegrave Pond.　WM

Priddy Lead Works showing three chimneys, the third being built in March 1908 shortly before the works were closed.　WM

Priddy Lead Works again showing three chimneys.　WM

The Lead Works possibly taken on the last day of production in May 1908. Bertie Weeks is by the smelter, Mark Lovell by the ingots, one of the men on the ramp is either the Mine Manager or Lord Waldegrave's agent.　BS

Albert Main at the plough.     DI

Horse ploughing, date unknown.     GB

Two gentlemen outside Manor Farm in the 1920s. The man on the right is James Maine, father of Albert, Arthur, Jim, Ern, Harry (who was killed in the Great War), Mary, Annie, Gilbert, Alice and Lilian.     HM & JD

Rose Farm in the late 1930s with Albert Main's wife, Evelyn, and son Jack before the move to Manor Farm, and Arthur's move from Manor Farm to Rose Farm.    HM & JD

Seymour King at Plummers Farm late 1930s, early 1940s. Left to right: ?, Will King, Mrs King senior, Katie King, Seymour King.    LS

Visit of a group of farmers to B.O.C.M., Avonmouth which included Jack Main (sixth from the left on the back row), Henry Dyke (to Jack's left), Bob Dyke (middle row fifth from the left), and Tommy Thompson (front row fifth from the left) who was the Waldegrave farm manager.    CD

Entente Cordiale in Priddy. Visiting French farmers standing in the garden in front of Manor Farm, organized by the Mid Somerset area N.F.U. in the mid 1960s. In the background can be seen Batch Cottage before any renovations.                    PM

Harold Baker and his son, Jim, with their tractor.
CM & LS

Forest Simmons on his tractor. His uncle Lillington Simmons had owned Laurel Cottage (later Laurel Farm) and part of what is now the Forge.
CM & LS

A photograph of farm workers around a tractor with Phyllis Sparkes (née Dyke) (Ashton's wife) on the tractor.      SS & AS

Seymour King milking, with Gary Sparkes looking on in about 1954.                                    LS

May Denly at Rowberrow Farm in 1960 feeding her hens.                                    NL

Cows at feed time at Rowberrow Farm in 1960.    NL

## How's that for prolificacy?

A fine set of quins born unaided to this Suffok x ewe. The lambs by a Suffolk ram were born on March 21st and were just three days old when this photograph was taken. They belong to Messrs. Sparkes & Brown of Castle Farm, East Harptree and the ewe was one of thirty purchased last September to be sold as couples in the Spring. The flock has been fed Sheldon Jones Ewe & Lamb nuts since late December.

Clipping from a farming journal in the 1980s.
Left to right: Ashton Sparkes, Mike Brown and Kevin Sparkes.                                    SS & AS

Robin Maine's cows going up the hill towards the Top Green after milking.
PM

Robin Maine with a calf at Manor Farm in 1998 being filmed for a children's television programme.
PM

Haymaking at Plummers Farm with Seymour King on the right.
LS

*Above & left*: Haymaking with Ashton Sparkes at Castle Farm in July 1950 with Marjorie, Frank, Carol, Susan, Bob and Bert – all Sparkes.

CD

Forest Simmons with friends from Hastings in front of his hayrick – and that is Clarice Main with a friend on the top.

CL & LM

The Main family haymaking in the field in front of the Church.

IW

Three gentleman rabbit catchers with their haul. They were probably men who came out from Bristol for a day's shooting.                                                                                              LS

Potato harvesting in the late 1950s.
Left to right:  Herbie Lovell, Albert Main, Robin Maine, Jack Main and
Arthur Wilkins.                                                                                                           HM & JD

A cow being dug out of a swallet in 1968.                                    SS & AS

Guarding the Christmas trees at Stockhill Woods.
Left to right: Jim Fowler, Maurice Winter, Ken Yarde who all worked for the Forestry Commission.
IW

Forestry Commission sign, with local office number, taken in 1988/90. CB

Forestry Commission/Contractor tractor in Stockhill Woods in 1988/90. CB

# CHAPTER 10

# Priddy and Hunting

*Left & below*: The Mendip Hunt Gymkhana held at Priddy Hill Farm in 1934.          AF

Digging out a fox in the field opposite Castle Farm c.1935.

SS &AS

The Mendip Hunt on Priddy Green showing the Joint Masters: Capt. Roland Corbett M.F.H. and Major S.C. Houston M.F.H.
AF

Captain and Mrs Firbank on Priddy Green in 1934/35.
AF

Mendip Hunt's first Meet of the year in 1934/35. The first Meet is always held on Priddy Green and the New Inn provides the 'Cup'.
AF

The Mendip Hunt Meet at the Castle of Comfort in 1934/35.
AF

The Mendip Hunt field and hounds moving off up Cheddar Gorge after a Meet at the Cliff Hotel in Cheddar Gorge c.1935.                    AF

The Mendip Hunt hounds being exercised  on the frozen Waldegrave Pool at Stockhill.           AF

The Mendip Hunt field and hounds  moving across Blackdown c.1935.                    AF

The Mendip Hunt hounds being exercised in front of Mrs Firbank's house at the Kennels c.1935.    AF

Wesley Voke competing in a Mendip Farmers Hunt Point-to-point.
BP

Ashton Sparkes as the Whipper-in (third horseman) with the Mendip Farmers Hunt in 1950. He spent five years with the Hunt after the War until his father's retirement from farming. The person in front appears to be Mrs Firbank and the Huntsman on the white horse is possibly Will Jackson.
CD

The hounds and field move off on a snowy winter's day in the early 1950s. The Whipper-in on the right is Ashton Sparkes.
SS & AS

*Below & right*: The Huntsman and Whipper-in taking the hounds to Wookey Hole, stopping for refreshments outside the Queen Victoria.

GB

*Above & left*: The Mendip Hunt Boxing Day Meet on the Green in the early 1970s.    GB

# CHAPTER 11

# Priddy and Leisure

## CAVING

This has become a central leisure activity on the Mendips, with Priddy having two of the finest caves in Eastwater Cavern and Swildon's Hole. It is so because of the early pioneers who explored the mysterious holes and swallets in the landscape. Today speleologists continue to explore and extend our knowledge of the hidden world in the Mendip limestone.

The entrance to Swildon's Hole c.1898 before the cave was explored. Photograph by Balch. DI

Eastwater Depression before the cave was opened c.1898. Photograph by Balch. DI

'Last Five Men Out' at Swildon's Hole dated 13 August 1921.
Left to right: Arthur Main, 'Holly', ? Simmons, Herbert Balch, Reg Balch. Photograph from J. Harry Savory Collection, Wells Museum. DI

The Old Grotto in Swildon's Hole, a party on 13 August 1921.
Left to right, back to front: Herbert Balch, Reg Balch, ?, Ayerst, Vicar, Quinn, Quinn, Ayerst, Edgar K. Tratman, Main, Higgins, Simmons, 'Holly'.

Photograph from J. Harry Savory Collection, Wells Museum.                    DI

Albert Main and Bertie Weeks building the entrance to Swildon's Hole in the 1960s.  BS

# SPORT

Priddy Football Team 1908 outside the Victoria Inn.
Left to right back: Tom Gadd, Wilf Weeks, Frank Weeks. Middle: Jack Weeks, Tom Bishop, Bert Weeks. Front: Art Payne, Tommie Jordan, Jim Main, Bert Payne, Albert Main.
GB

Another Priddy Football Team, again early twentieth Century. GB

The Queen Victoria Cricket Team in 1979 organized by Nick Leyton and Norman Chivers which became very enthusiastic for a few years, entering the Village Knockout Championship and actually winning one. They played in one of Norman Chivers' fields as you approach the top of Deer Leap. In that field is an old cobbled Dewpond where young people used to go fishing for roach and large newts.
Left to right, back: Dave Inwood, Jeremy Barnes, Peter Izard, Stuart Kerton, Stephen Main. Front: 'Ev', Elaine Loxton, 'Mini' Maxwell, Norman Chivers, Judy Baynes, Alun Jenkins.

# SCOUTS

For many years Priddy had a thriving Scout Troop – the 1st Priddy. Alfred Lovell was Scout Master when Maurice Winter joined in 1927. He was succeeded by Bob Dyke who was Scout Leader for many years and he was aided by Roger Dors. It faded in the late 1950s / early 1960s.

Scouts parading outside the Church with Bob Dyke as Scout Leader. The original banner was kindly given by Bob Dyke for display in the Church and can be seen there today. BS

Maurice Winter's Scout Certificate in 1927 when he was thirteen. IW

Scouts outside the Village Hall in the 1950s. BS

Four photographs of the Priddy Scout Troop during the late 1940s and early 1950s when entering floats at Jamborees. Familiar faces include Charlie Lovell, Robin Maine, Bob Dyke.     CD

# ENTERTAINMENT

Priddy Folk have always found a way to enjoy life and entertain themselves and others.

Wells Carnival Night in the 1940s showing members of the Priddy float: Grace Weeks, Bella Holder, Georgina Lane, Mrs French and Lena Simmons.   CM & LS

Priddy Footlights after a performance, probably held in the School in 1949.   BS

Chris Dyke and friends organized a children's charity fête in July 1961 which was held in the garden of Lower Pitts Bungalow, now Badgers Wood.   CD

Bevis Miller and Jacky Carter at Priddy Folk Fayre in 1998. They began the Folk Fayre in 1990, with the School PTA, as a fund raising event to provide a playground for the School. It has since grown and now involves many people from the village, and many more from away. It raises money for all village organizations as well as helping the School provide music for the children. Photograph Mid Somerset Newspapers.
GM

Priddy School children Maypole dancing at Priddy Folk Fayre in 1998. Photograph Mid Somerset Newspapers.
GM

# RALLIES

The Village Green frequently hosts meetings and this photograph shows vintage cars with members of the Baynes family in one during the 1980s.

GB

Maurice and Iris Winter and Roy Denly on the Green during a gathering of vintage tractors during the early 1990s.

HRA

# THE SILVER SCREEN

Over the years the environs of Priddy have been a popular location for film and television productions. Watch out for the view from the top of Ebbor Gorge out across the Levels in *The Remains of the Day*.

*Robin Hood* being filmed at Blackrock during the mid 1980s.
GB

In 1983 Wendy Richards visited the Queen Victoria Inn for the day whilst shooting for a series of television programmes about famous people's obsessions. Wendy's particular interest was frogs and she was taken to a pond locally to catch some – it is thought the series was not too successful.
GB

Panorama shot of the period production, *Berkeley Square*, being made for television on the Green in 1997.
SS & AS

# CHAPTER 12

# Priddy Friendly Society

Once meeting in the Queen Victoria, the Friendly Society is now based on the New Inn. With its long tradition of serving the needs of the villagers, it continues to celebrate its existence annually with its Muster and Roll Call, parade to the Church, a service, lunch in the Village Hall and an afternoon of sports. Through much of the last century this took place at Whitsun.

A Memorial Service to H.M. King Edward VII in Priddy in May 1910.

DI

Bucket Tilting on the Green during the Friendly Society Club Day in 1931. Jack Main is in a raincoat and sou'wester about to attempt the tilt without getting wet! Note the large hurdle stack in the background.

HM & JD

Priddy Friendly Society Club Day during the time of no band with a car leading the group with a loud speaker for the music; by Church Farm.    DP

The Priddy Tug of War Team with coach, Ivor Payne.
From the front:    Trevor Dunford, Terry Newton, Norman Sainsbury, Bob Brown, David Neale, Norman Parfitt, Dennis Payne, Eric Dors.    DP

Lewis Weeks with the Friendly Society Banner and Company on Club Day outside the Church in the early 1960s.    DP

Priddy Friendly Society parading to Church in 1970. Bertie Weeks is carrying the Banner.                NL

Friendly Society Club Day outside the Church 1971. The oldest member of the Society, Bertie Weeks holding the Staff, is shown with the youngest member at the time, Keith Payne.
Back left to right: Maurice Winter, ??, Roger Dors, Dave Searle, Alan Thomas, Gilbert Lane, Richard Golding, Bert Body, ??, Chris Weeks, Jim Parfitt    Middle left to right: Chris Winter, ??, Fred Payne, ??, Bertie Weeks, Bob Sparkes, Lewis Weeks   Boys in the front left to right:  Wesley Lane, Barry Payne, Keith Payne, Kevin Sparkes.                FP, TP & IW

Skittles on the Green in the 1970s during the Friendly Society Club Day, including Pete Body (playing), Chris, Maurice and Iris Winter, Mabel Payne, Helen Parfitt, Karen Parfitt.                    DP

The Friendly Society Club Day outside the Church in 1973 with Lewis Weeks holding the Banner and Roger Dors holding the Staff.

Main body left to right: Alan Thomas, Dave Searle, Ashton Sparkes, Jack Main, Bob Sparkes, Roy Denley, Fred Payne, David Neale, Jim Parfitt, Mr Harding, Lewis Weeks, Jim ? (David Neales's uncle), John Davis, Nick Leyton, Roger Dors, Robin Maine, Julian Leyton, ??, Richard Golding, Revd. Denis Smith

Front left to right:  Jeremy Barnes, Daren Barnes, Stephen Main, Chris Winter, Kevin Sparkes, Barry Payne, Keith Payne.                    IW

The Friendly Society Club Day marching to the Church in the pouring rain in 1979 with Denis Payne holding the Banner.
IW

The Friendly Society in 1980 marching up to the Church with Fred Payne leading the way with one of the Banners. In the background Bob Sparkes carries the other Banner.
IW

The Priddy Friendly Society have their Club Day each year on the May Bank Holiday, nearest Whitsun. The Monday always includes an afternoon of sports on the Green. This is an example in about 1980 showing Julie Rackstraw and Nikki Gwyther.
JR

The Friendly Society in 1982 outside the Church with Bob Sparkes and Fred Payne holding the Banners. Also seen are Ashton Sparkes, Lewis Weeks, Nick Leyton, Peter Leyton, Stephen Main, Keith Payne, Jack Main, Elliot Davis, Michael Main, Peter Pearson, Matthew Pearson, Kevin Sparks, Chris Winter, Jonathon Pearson and Barry Payne.   IW

The Friendly Society in 1983, the Centenary Year, showing Norman Mullis reading the roll call and Fred Payne and Bob Sparkes holding the Banners and Richard Leyton holding the Staff.   Also can be seen Christopher Thompson, Jack Maine and Ashton Sparkes in their caps, Barry Jenkins, Michael Main, Stephen Main, James Furze, Chris Winter, Keith Payne, Nick Leyton, Mike Garfield, Barry Payne, Peter Leyton and Kevin Sparkes.   IW

The Friendly Society in 1986 showing Norman Mullis reading the roll call and Fred Payne and Bob Sparkes holding the Banners.   Also can be seen are Mike Brown, Nick Leyton, Chris Winter, Maurice Winter, Mike Garfield, Nick Furze, Peter Pearson, James Furze, Robin Maine and Richard Golding.   IW

The Friendly Society Club Day in about 1987 showing the Tug of War at the end of the afternoon of sports.    PM

The Friendly Society in 1987 showing Alan Thomas reading the roll call and Fred Payne and Bob Sparkes hold the banners.
Left to right:  Bob Dyke, Keith Payne, Roger Dors, Mark Glover, Matthew Pearson, Fred Payne, Alan Thomas, Chris Winter, Roy Denley, Mark Golding, Phil Hendy, Maurice Winter, Jim Speed, ??, Ashton Sparkes, Bob Sparkes, Steve Sparkes, Arthur Speed, Barry Wilton, Mr Jarratt Snr, Frank Cook, Tony Jarratt.    IW

The Friendly Society sports afternoon in 1990/91.    GB

The Friendly Society sports afternoon in 1994.                    JR

The Priddy Friendly Society organize a Guy Fawkes night on the Green each year, with a bonfire, fireworks and hot-dogs.  This was taken in 1998 and if you look you can see the trees around the Green silhouetted by the fireworks.                    SS & AS

A sequence of four photos. The Priddy Friendly Society collecting and erecting a very large Christmas tree to put on the Green in 1998, showing Nick Furze and Tim Andrews with Barry Payne and his lorry.

SS & AS

The Millennium Children's Party held in the Village Hall on 1 January 2000 given by the Friendly Society.    PM

# CHAPTER 13

# Priddy Fair

The origins of Priddy Fair are not clear. Traditionally it is thought the Fair moved from Wells to Priddy during the Black Death in 1348. However, there is evidence that a Fair existed before this date and it is thought that the Fair in Wells and the Priddy Fair joined together at that time – hence the question was it a sheep fair or a cloth fair. In its time it has been a fair for hoofed animals, and at the turn of the nineteenth century horses were in abundance, unsurprisingly as they were the prime means of transport. Priddy Fair then was the annual opportunity to trade-in your steed for a new one. Today it is now held on the Wednesday nearest the 21 August although originally it was held on the feast of St Lawrence the Martyr which is 10 August.

Priddy Fair in 1908 looking across to Fountain Cottage.                                    DI

Priddy Fair in 1908 viewed from Solomon Coomb.
DI

Priddy Fair in 1908 showing the Guardians of the Peace. As tradition has it, there has always been the promise of trouble at the Fair.          CM & LS

Two views of Priddy Fair
between 1911 and 1925      WM

Two more views of Priddy Fair
between 1911 and 1925.      WM

Priddy Fair on 21 August 1916 looking across the Green towards the Batch. Note the cottage at the top of the Little Batch. WM

Priddy Fair again early in the twentieth century to judge by the bowler hats. CM & LS

Priddy Fair in 1928 showing lots of horses in the foreground and sheep in front of St Cuthbert's Farm wall. Ashton Sparkes remembers this Fair – he was ten years old. CM & LS

THE BOOK OF PRIDDY

Hurdles being erected on the green. In earlier years they were used from the stack for the sheep and were put back after the Fair and re-thatched.          HM & JD

Priddy Sheep Fair in the 1950s.          CM & LS

Priddy Sheep Fair in the 1950s and in the background on the right hand side, a rare glimpse of the temporary hostels for the land girls in one of St Cuthbert's fields bordering the green.          CM & LS

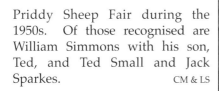

Priddy Sheep Fair during the 1950s. Of those recognised are William Simmons with his son, Ted, and Ted Small and Jack Sparkes.          CM & LS

The Coles family have been bringing their Fun Fair to Priddy Sheep Fair for very many  years and in the past have made Priddy their holiday destination. Here is the gondola ride in 1971 or 1972.    PM

Carolyne, Stephen and Michael Main on the gondolas brought by Coles Fun Fair at Priddy Sheep Fair in 1971 or 1972.    PM

Priddy Fair on a fine Wednesday 20 August 1980.  The auctioneer is on a cart in the background on the left.

AT

Priddy Fair in 1980  showing the sale of miscellaneous items.    AT

A gypsy showing off his horse at Priddy Fair during the mid 1990s.                    HRA

Gilbert Francis James Main, Hilda Main and Gilbert Jonathan Main (Pop) at Priddy Fair c.1990. Photograph from Mid Somerset Newspapers.    CM & LS

Fun fairs have changed, even if sheep haven't.  This is Priddy Fair in 1998.                    CM & LS

# CHAPTER 14

# The Villagers

The nearest available Census to 1900, that of 1891, for Priddy Parish, a far smaller parish than today, shows that 200 people lived in Priddy. The most frequently appearing surnames were: Weeks 42, Simmons 12, Savage 11, Speed, 11, Main 9, Hann 9, Vincent 8, Pain 8 and Pitman 7.

Gilbert John (always known as Jack) Main in his christening gown at Rose Farm c.1912.          HM & JD

Mr and Mrs Dyke senior with six children, including Bob front right. Henry is the curly-haired lad in the middle, Phyllis is the youngest girl in the front. The Dykes had come to Priddy from Sturminster Newton in Dorset.          SS & AS

A procession of men going to vote in Westbury-sub-Mendip on 21 January 1910.          LS

Wesley Voke, later to farm at Wills Farm, with his bicycle outside Manor Farm.    BP

Priddy Friendly Society Club Day Band in the 1920s.  The lady on the left is Beatrice Payne.    BP

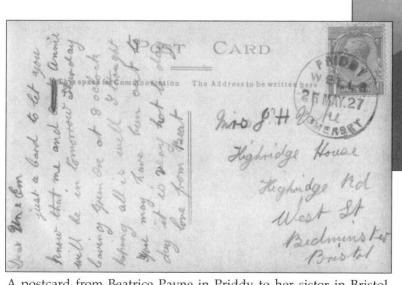

A postcard from Beatrice Payne in Priddy to her sister in Bristol informing her of her arrival in Bristol the next day.  She would have walked to Green Ore and caught the bus.  The post office at that time was at No. 2 Pin Cross.    BP

Ashton Sparkes in 1933/35. Ashton recalls that as one of the oldest pupils at the School, aged twelve to fourteen years, it was his duty to collect water from the Fountain each morning for the hot drinks. He never missed a day's schooling and has a certificate to that effect.  Elsie Lovell (now Elsie Speed) also got good attendance certificates.    SS & AS

Stanley Russell and Gladys Payne on their wedding day in 1949. The pageboy is Bob Sparkes aged seven.    BS

Blodwen Russell (known as May) and Bert Sparkes on their wedding day in the 1930s. The bridesmaids are Rene Neil, Kathleen Sparkes (later to marry Bob Dyke) and Miss Gadd.

BS

The Sparkes family taken in the School playground, probably at a wedding. Left to right back: Wilf, Bert, Frank, Ashton, Vernon. Front: Kathleen, John, Mabel, Ethel.    BS

Albert and Evelyn Main at the back door of Manor Farm, Albert having just come in from working with the horses.  HM & JD

Robin Maine in scout uniform in June 1949.  CD

Wilf Sparkes' first car at Castle Farm.  CD

Roger Dors, the present proprietor, outside the Hunter's Lodge aged ten in 1949 on his pony Spider.  RD

Maurice Winter and Alfred Lovell (Iris Winter's father) in his Scout Master's hat in 1949.  IW

Outside the cowsheds at Lower Pitts Farm showing Henry Dyke (in the trilby), Robert Dyke senior and Robert Dyke junior (Bob). The man on the right is unknown.                                                    CD

Fred and Shirley Payne sometime during the 1950s before they were married. The Ford 10 van belonged to Bob Sparkes.                                                    BS

Albert Main with Prince. Christine, Archie, Jennifer and a friend are on board.                          HM & JD

Jack and Hilda Main's family outside Solomon Coombe. Left to right, back: Hilda, Mary, Robin, Jack. Front: Jenny, Christine, Audrey.          HM & JD

Seymour King while he was a tenant at Plummers Farm. The year is unknown but he always looked the same and was a familiar figure walking with his dog well into the 1980s.                          GB

On the Green with the New Inn in the background. Left to right: Kate Winter (Maurice's mother), Ken Payne, Jim Speed (Elsie's husband), Wesley Simmons, ?, Mrs Pop (Lena) Simmons, ?.　IW

A social event in a marquee in the village in 1953, possibly a wedding, which includes Ruth Baker, Gilbert Lane and Ted Simmons　CM & LS

Lewis Weeks and Denis Payne in about 1954 with the Friendly Society Banner.　DP

Robin Maine, Pamela Phillips in 1958 before they were married with Bob the dog. Photographed outside Solomon Coombe with the Vicarage in the background.　DP

Roy and May Denly at Rowberrow Farm in 1960. They bought the farm in 1959 and stayed there until 1965 during which time they did a milk round locally.

NL

Robert and Ida Maud Dyke at Lower Pitts Farm on their Golden Wedding day in 1959/60. CD

The whole of the Dyke Family at Lower Pitts Farm celebrating Robert and Ida's Golden Wedding. Left to right back row: Henry Dyke, ?, Gordon Rogers, Jim Maidment with Derek and David Maidment. 3rd row: Ashton Sparkes, ?,?,?, Mr Beacham, Olive Maidment, Rosemary Beacham, Kathleen Dyke, ?. 2nd row includes Robert Dyke on the far right next to Aunty Flo and Mrs Beacham 4th from the right. Front row: Michael Beacham, Chris Dyke, Ida and Robert Dyke, Liz Beacham and Richard Beacham. CD

P.C. Jerry Brice, the Community Village Policeman, based at Chewton Mendip, outside the Queen Victoria Inn on his recently acquired motor bike c.1966. NL

Albert Main with his great-grandson, Stephen Main, returning from feeding the orphan lambs in 1967.  PM

Robert Phillip Henry Dyke on 30 October 1969 aged ninety years, six months.  SS & AS

A group of the Dors family taken outside the Hunter's Lodge in 1970 when Diana Dors was visiting.   Left to right back: Valerie Barnes (nee Dors), Tommy Barnes, Alan Lake, Valerie Dors, baby Jason Dors, Eric Dors (Roger's brother), baby Simon Dors, Phyllis Dors (Roger's mother), Jackie Dors.  Front: Jeremy and Darren Barnes, Diana's son, Diana Dors with Jason, Diana's other son, Ben Dors (Roger's father) and Helen Dors.

RD

Four generations of the Main family in 1970.
Left to right: Stephen (great-grandson), Albert, Robin
(grandson) and Jack (son).                    HM & JD

Geoff and Judy Baynes with Silver on their wedding
day in October 1970.                    GB

Silver, the Baynes' family pony, found his way home
alone early one Sunday morning, after a gymkhana in
Burcott the previous day. It was claimed he was
homesick and impatient for his pint c.1970.    GB

The Playgroup run by Ann Thompson in the Forge having a morning out in the snow in 1974. Left to right: Laurie Gwyther, Richard Leyton, Nikki Gwyther, Iain Thompson, Tracey Payne, Lucy Davis and Rachel Dors. HM & JD

Priddy Playgroup in the Village Hall in 1977.
Left to right, back: Deborah Squires, Ben Butterell, Peter Murrell, Roby Godwin, Debbie Lewer, Hans Richard Campbell, Catherine Gibbons, Ruth Moysey. Middle: Laurie Gwyther, Dan Butterell, Jake Baynes, Dean Sparkes, Julie Rackstraw, Nicola Baynes, Lucy Davis, Tracey Payne. Front: Nikki Gwyther, Daisy Pomeroy, Richard Leyton, James Furze (floor), Carl Campbell, Mark Golding, Rachel Dors, Daniel Moysey. AT

The Silver Jubilee Beard Growing Competition in 1977.
Left to right, back: Ray Andrews, Bob Murrell, Robin Maine, Jack Phillips, Robin Butterell, Geoff Baynes, Tom Tucker. Front: Fred Payne, the lady who presented the prizes, Roger Dors, ? PM

Ann and Albert Thompson and Geoff and Judy Baynes in Scandanavian ski mode 1980/81 outside the Queen Victoria Inn. GB

Priddy Friendly Society Sports Committee Secretary, Chris Winter, presents cheques for £150 to Brenda Finlayson, Headmistress of the School, and Bob Sparkes, Chairman of the Village Hall Committee, at the New Inn on 12 October 1981. Also in the picture are Nick Leyton, Chairman of the Friendly Society, and Fred Payne.

IW

Jack Foxwell, well-known local character and brother of Walter Foxwell. Jack lived at what is now the Research Station at Wells Hill Bottom with his family. As a widower he lived in a caravan at Eastwater Farm. He renovated and rebuilt a number of dry stone walls in the village and this photograph shows him with his work at the Queen Victoria Inn.     GB

The Deputy Premier of Australia, Malcolm Bryce, made frequent visits to London but had seen nothing of England and determined to put this right. During a visit to Cheddar in 1983 he paid a visit to the Queen Victoria Inn as an example of a typical English country pub.     GB

A group of Priddy children in Wells' Market Place on a Scout Fun Run in 1984. They are Jake Baynes, Iain Thompson, James Furze, Richard Leyton, Antony and Julie Rackstraw, Laurie and Nikki Gwyther and Daniel Butterell.   NF

Priddy children after the Fun Run. Left to right: Daniel Butterell, Iain Thompson, Jake Baynes, James Furze and Richard Leyton.   NF

Reg Payne with his cat outside the back door of St Cuthbert's Farm where he lived.   HRA

The Chewton Evergreens visiting Chewton Mendip Primary School. Those from Priddy were Jack Furze, Vera Inwood, George Hopkins, Mary Davis, Hilda Main, Bob Dyke and Elsie Speed. On the bench is Jane Hack, the Headmistress, with some children from her top class.     CD

Four generations: Mrs Gladys Phillips, her daughter Mrs Pamela Maine, her daughter Carolyne Hares and her daughter, Camilla.
PM

Hilda Main and Bob Dyke, Priddy's Church Wardens, outside Wells Cathedral after receiving the Maundy Money from the Queen at the Maundy Money Service in 1993.     CD

Maurice Winter with his broom outside Pincross on the Green late 1980s.     HRA

Dean Sparkes' wedding in 1993.
Left to right: Kevin Sparkes, Tim Boady, Dean Sparkes, Mark Golding and Lee Sparkes.

LS

Arthur Blaymires ran the Deer Leap School of Motoring from the village in the 1990s. This photograph was taken in 1994 prior to the hurdle stack restoration.

AB

To mark the Millennium the Priddy Friendly Society organised a gathering of the present and former village inhabitants for a photograph. On 31 December 1999 the village gathered in Solomon Coomb and Max Jones mounted a scaffold tower to capture this unique record. The Friendly Society presented all in the photograph with a copy together with an identification index.

# Subscribers

Gordon and Julie Airey, Nottingham
Robin J. Ames, Priddy, Somerset
Ruud Mantingh and Yasmin Stockwell, Priddy, Somerset
Mrs Judy, Mr Tim, and Lucy-Rose Andrews, Priddy, Somerset
Mr and Mrs Attwood, Priddy, Somerset
A. M. Barlow MRCVS and Mrs Jeannie Barlow, Rookham, Wells, Somerset
Jeremy Barnes, formerly of Priddy
Valerie A. Barnes, Midsomer Norton, Bath
Tina Bath, Priddy, Somerset
Judy and Geoffrey Baynes, Priddy, Somerset
Stuart and Karin Baynes, Johannesburg, South Africa
Jake Baynes, Priddy, Somerset
Dennis and Rita Beckett, Priddy, Somerset
Arthur E. Blaymires, Wells, somerset
Christine Bourne, Westbay, Dorset
Jim and Marion Boyd, Sycamore House, Priddy, Somerset
Lee Brooks
Rachel and Andy Buckle, Gloucs
Daniel Butterell
Ben Butterell
Gemma Butterell
Robin Butterell
Penny Butterell
Jean V. Case (nee Gadd), Shepton Mallet, Somerset
Mr K and Mrs C Clark, Westbury Sub Mendip, Somerset
Henry and Sheila Clark, Priddy, Somerset
David R. Coles, Priddy, Somerset
Dean and Glenda Collier, Priddy
Leonard Cooksley, Felton, Backwell
Tony and Indra Cotton, Priddy, Somerset
May Denly, Priddy, Somerset
Rachel A. Dors, Priddy, Somerset
Bryan R. Dors, Wells, Somerset
Eric (Ner) Dors, Hunters lodge Inn, Priddy, Somerset
R. G. and J. A. Dors, Priddy, Somerset
Christine Duckett, Priddy, Somerset
Imogen Duncan, Street, Somerset
J. Eagar, Ston Easton
Justine and Mark Emery, Priddy
Fear, Priddy, Somerset
Brenda and Jim Finlayson, Priddy, Somerset
A. Firbank, Priddy
Tim Francis, Richmond, Surrey
Helen R. Frayne, Wells, Somerset
Ken Freston, Priddy, Somerset
Fry, The Stirrup Cup
Catherine and James Furze
Nick and Veronica Furze
Raymond L. Gadd, Warrington, Cheshire
I. R. and D. E. Gibbons, Priddy, Somerset
Mrs A. J. Gibbons, Priddy, Somerset
Eric Gibbs, Wookey Hole, Somerset
Joan and Peter Goddard, Mendip Caving Group, Nordrach, Somerset
Richard and Pauline Golding, Priddy
Mark Golding, Rodney Stoke
Nicola Grass, Draycott, Somerset
Richard Green, Wells, Somerset
John C. R. Griffiths, Priddy, Somerset
John and Mary Gwyther, Priddy, Somerset
Julie Hares, Shepton Mallet
Kevin Heaton and Rhona Gauld, Priddy, Somerset
P. G. Hendy, Evercreech, Somerset
Julie Hesketh, Mendip Caving Group, London
Maurice and Judy Hewins, Wessex Cave Club
Sue and Ian Horn, Priddy, Somerset
Susan E. Humber, Wellington Farm, Priddy
Vera Innwood and George Hopkins, Wookey Hole, Somerset

David J. Irwin, Priddy, Somerset
Jane Jarratt, Draycott, Somerset
Tony Jarratt, Priddy, Somerset
Margaret Jennings, Priddy, Somerset
Karen and Barry Jones, Butcombe, Somerset
Andy Keys-Toyer, Rookham Hill
Gilbert George Lane, Marston Lane, Frome, Somerset
Stephen and Linda LeFevre, Priddy, Somerset
Richard Leyton, London W12
Nick, Pauline, Richard and Peter Leyton, Priddy, Somerset
Robert Long, Frenchay, Bristol
Keith Long, Frenchay, Bristol
Heather A. Mackay, Wookey Hole, Somerset
Father Ewan A. Macpherson
Mary Main, Alberta, Canada
Stephen P. Main, Manor Farm, Priddy
Hilda Main and Jenny Davis, Priddy, Somerset
Mendip Caving Group, Nordrach, Somerset
The Moysey Family, Bratton Clovelly
(Priddy 1970-80)
Louise and Bob Murrell, Wells, Somerset
Lee Neale, Darshill, Somerset
Julia Nest, Priddy, Somerset
Ted and Ruth Nest, Priddy, Somerset
Mark and Sally Osborne, Charmouth, Dorset
Martin Owen, Priddy, Somerset
Michael Owen, Priddy, Somerset
Tom and Ann Owen, Priddy, Somerset
Stuart and Sheila Palmer, Priddy, Somerset
Dawn Paul
Marie E. Payne, Priddy, Somerset
Shirley Payne
Barry Payne
Dennis Payne, Priddy, Somerset
Keith Payne
Tracey Payne
Elizabeth Payton
J. C. Peacock
Bridgitte Perkins, Priddy, Somerset
B.E and B. D Prewer, Priddy, Somerset
John and Jean Rackstraw, Priddy, Somerset
Antony Rackstraw and Rebecca Thornborough, Draycott, Somerset
Jane and Charles Ranaboldo,
Bob Reynolds, Priddy, Somerset
Jonathan Roberts, Wanstrow, Somerset
J. Rowlinson (nee Gadd), Vartegg, S. Wales
Audrey Ryall, Shepton Mallet, Somerset
Ivan Sandford, Priddy, Somerset
Nicola and Mat Sibley, Cowplain, Waterlooville, Hampshire
Miss L. Simmons
Dean Sparkes, Priddy, Somerset
Stephen A. Sparkes, Priddy, Somerset
Gary Vernon Sparkes, Priddy, Somerset
Lee Gary Sparkes, Priddy, Somerset
Lesley Sparkes, Priddy, Somerset
Robin, Valerie, Anthony and Deborah Squires, Residents 1974-1986
Malcolm and Jackie Tarrant, Priddy, Somerset
Mavis Taviner, West Harptree
Royston Uphill, Chewton Mendip
Elizabeth T. Walker, Priddy, Somerset
John F. W. Walling, Newton Abbot, Devon
Mr A and Mrs P Watson, Priddy, Somerset
Miss J Watson, Cheddar, Somerset
Wendy Weeks, East Harptree
Anne and Doug Weston,
Jon and Mel Wheatley,
Iris W. Winters,